Pastry Without Tears

Donna Thacker
Pastry Without Tears

Illustrated by David Shaw

D.A. Cameron
Ottawa

Created and prepared
for publication at
D.A. Cameron Books
14-39 Putman Avenue
Ottawa, Ontario
Canada

Canadian Cataloguing in Publication Data

Thacker, Donna, 1943-
  Pastry without tears

ISBN 0-9691315-1-8

1. Pastry   I. Shaw, David, 1947-
II. Title.

TX763.T53 1986   641.8'65   C86-090093-2

Contents

For Blaine
whose birthday cake is always
apple pie

How to Use This Book to Solve the Riddle of Pastry

Begin with **The Basic Recipe** and the first part of the riddle is solved—lard plus flour, salt and water equal pastry. Delightfully simple! And just like Mother, **Pastry Without Tears** uses a magic ingredient—*Tenderflake* lard. (My Mother and I have used *Tenderflake* for 52 years!)

Move step by step through **The Technique** section. And you quickly find how to squeeze, sprinkle and squish the ingredients together. Squishing and squeezing used to be a no no but **Pastry Without Tears** uses ingredients that love to be squeezed!

With your perfect 'hamburger' of pastry turn to **Pastry Shapes** ranging from the simplest *Lady in Bikini* to *Pears in Overcoats* to *Chocolate Strawberry Baskets*.

As you taste your first *flaky* treat (while curled up in a fat armchair) you will know that Mother was right, a piece of pie and a glass of milk make everything right with the world!

Thanks to Mother, Richard Taylor, Jane Crosbie,
Denise Davidson, Patricia McColl Bee,
my husband Blaine, son Todd and daughter Tynan
for:

    waiting
    gently pushing
    helping
    watching
    and dreaming!

When someone gives you pleasure
you want not only to share the moments
but to mention their names.

The Basic Recipe

For one pie:

2 cups	all purpose flour	
1 cup	pastry flour	
1 teaspoon	salt	
1 cup	*Tenderflake* lard	cold
2 tablespoons	*Tenderflake* lard	cold
½ cup	water	

The Squeeze Test on "One of Those Days"...

The Basic Technique by Hand

1. Choose a large bowl.
   Add the flours and salt.
   Stir the flour mixture.

2. Cut the 1 cup lard into ¼″ squares.
   Sprinkle the squares on the flour mixture.
   Work the lard and flour mixture together.
   Use your hands. (The mixture will now look like coarse bread crumbs!)
   Now give the flour mixture the *Squeeze Test*!

   ### The Squeeze Test
   Take a handful of flour mixture and squeeze firmly. The mixture should form a clump now that holds together easily. But flour is funny; on some days, the mixture will hold together at this point and on other days it won't. If it is "one of those days" the mixture will fall apart. Now the 2 tablespoons of lard you have left comes in handy! Add this lard one tablespoon at a time, until you declare the mixture to be *perfect* — forming a clump that holds together easily.

3. Fill an empty salt shaker with the water.
   Sprinkle the water all over the flour mixture.

4. Stir the flour mixture 6 or 7 times. (Resist stirring any more, as
   the pastry will become too tough.)

5. Pour the pastry into a large plastic bag.
   Squeeze the pastry into a ball.

PASTRY IN A PLASTIC BAG...

6. Flatten the ball into a hamburger shape.
   Place in the refrigerator.
   Leave for ½ hour.
   or
   Leave overnight.

7. Leave the pastry for 40 minutes on the table if it was in the refrigerator overnight.
Use your hands to flatten the hamburger shape until it is ½″ thick.

8. Remove the pastry from the plastic bag.

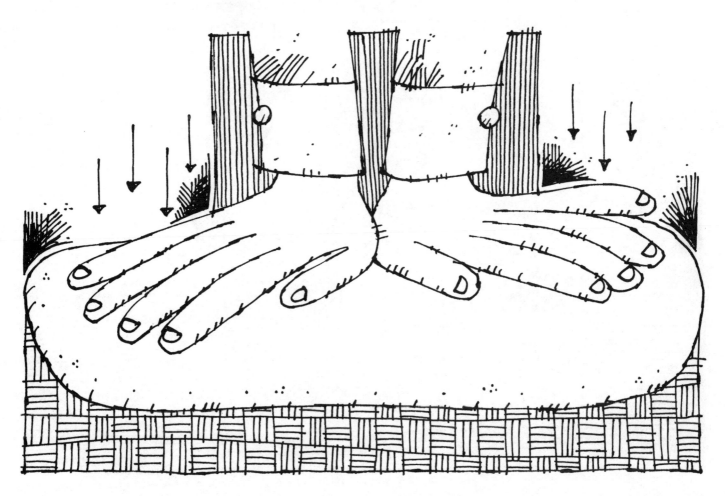

9. Now you are ready to make one of the pastry treats!
   See *Pastry Shapes* page 27.
   Begin with the easier shapes starting on page 28 and work to
   the end of the book where the special pastry treats are!

The Basic Technique by Food Processor

1. Use the metal blade.
   Add the flours and salt to the work bowl.

2. Cut the 1 cup lard into ¼″ squares.

3. Add the squares to the work bowl.
   Turn the food processor on and off quickly 10 times.
   Now give the flour mixture the *Squeeze Test*!

   The Squeeze Test
   Take a handful of flour mixture and squeeze firmly. The
   mixture should form a clump now that holds together easily.
   But flour is funny; on some days, the mixture will hold
   together at this point and on other days it won't. If it is "one of
   those days" the mixture will fall apart. Now the 2 tablespoons
   of lard you have left comes in handy. Add this lard one
   tablespoon at a time, turn the food processor on and off
   quickly 2 or 3 times, until you declare the mixture to be
   perfect — forming a clump that holds together easily.

4. Pour in the water.
    Turn the food processor on and off quickly 10 times ONLY.
    Resist turning the food processor on any more, as the pastry
    will become too tough.

5. Pour the pastry into a large plastic bag.
   Squeeze the pastry into a ball.

6. Flatten the ball into a hamburger shape.
   Place in the refrigerator.
   Leave for ½ hour.
   or
   Leave overnight.

7. Leave the pastry for 40 minutes on the table if it was in the refrigerator overnight.
   Use your hands to flatten the hamburger shape until it is ½″ thick.

8. Remove the pastry from the plastic bag.

9. Now you are ready to make one of the pastry treats.
   See *Pastry Shapes* page 27.
   Begin with the easier shapes starting on page 28 and work to
   the end of the book where the special pastry treats are!

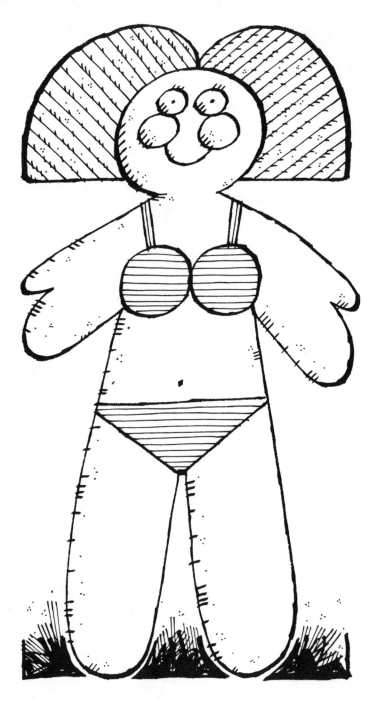

Lady in Bikini

You need the basic recipe ingredients.

Follow the basic technique until you have completed step 8 by hand or step 8 by food processor.

Now:
Grease two cookie pans and dust with flour.
Dust your rolling pin with flour.
Divide the pastry in half.
Use your rolling pin to roll pastry directly on the pans until 1/8" thick. Turn the pastry over three or four times as you roll.
Cut into lady shapes. Use a wax paper pattern like the one on this page as your guide.
Use a fork to 'draw' in her bikini.
Use a pen top to cut eyes and cheeks.
Place the pans in the refrigerator.
Leave for 15 minutes.

Heat oven to 425°.
Bake one pan on the middle rack for about 10 minutes. (Let the other pan wait and cook later on the middle rack.)
Leave lady on her pan.
Leave for 5 minutes on a cooling rack.
Remove lady from her pan and return to the cooling rack for 10 minutes.

Gingerbread Boy Garland

You need the basic recipe ingredients plus

milk
sugar or tiny decorating candies

Follow the basic technique until you have completed step 8 by hand or step 8 by food processor.

Now:
Grease two cookie pans and dust with flour.
Dust your rolling pin with flour.
Divide the pastry in half.
Use your rolling pin to roll pastry directly on the pans until 1/8" thick. Turn the pastry over three or four times as you roll.
Cut into gingerbread boy shapes with a cookie cutter. (Cut the shapes about 2" apart as they 'grow' in the oven!)
Place the pans in the refrigerator.
Leave for 15 minutes.

Heat oven to 425°.
Brush the gingerbread boys with milk and sprinkle quickly with sugar or tiny decorating candies.
Bake one pan on the middle rack for about 10 minutes. (Let the other pan wait and cook later on the middle rack.)
Leave boys on their pan.
Leave for 5 minutes on a cooling rack.
Remove boys from their pan and return to the cooling rack for 10 minutes.

Lay gingerbread boys in garland shapes, as in the drawing.

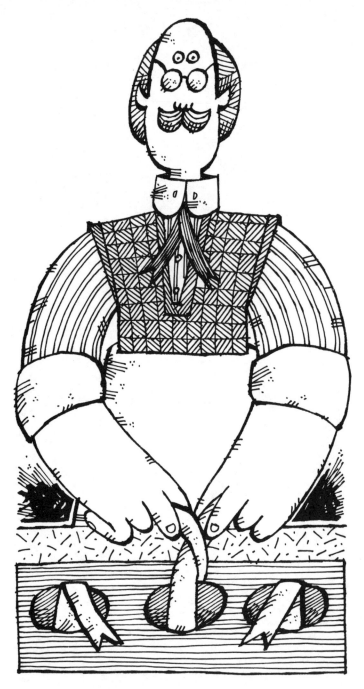

Sausage in Ribbons

You need the basic recipe ingredients plus

> caraway or poppy seeds
> smoked cocktail sausages, 20

Make this change to the basic recipe:

> Add 1 tablespoon caraway or poppy seeds to the flour

Follow the basic technique until you have completed step 8 by hand or step 8 by food processor.

Now:
Dampen your table with water.
Lay two large pieces of wax paper on the table. (The water helps the wax paper to stick to the table.)
Dust the wax paper with flour.
Dust your rolling pin with flour.
Divide the pastry in half.
Use your rolling pin to roll pastry directly on the wax paper until ⅛" thick. Turn the pastry over three or four times as you roll.
Cut into strips ½" wide. Use a tape measure ½" wide as your guide.
Cut each strip into 8" lengths.
Take hold of each end of a strip and tie around a smoked cocktail sausage.

Place the sausages in ribbons about 1" apart on cookie pans.
Place the pans in the refrigerator.
Leave for 15 minutes.

Heat oven to 425°.
Bake one pan on the middle rack for about 10 minutes. (Let the other pan wait and cook later on the middle rack.)
Leave ribbons on their pan.
Leave for 5 minutes on a cooling rack.
Remove ribbons from their pan and return to the cooling rack for 10 minutes.

Walnut Bowties

You need the basic recipe ingredients plus

> walnuts, ground
> icing sugar
> cinnamon

Follow the basic technique until you have completed step 8 by hand or step 8 by food processor.

Now:
Dampen your table with water.
Lay two large pieces of wax paper on the table. (The water helps the wax paper to stick to the table.)
Dust the wax paper with flour.
Dust your rolling pin with flour.
Divide the pastry in half.
Use your rolling pin to roll pastry directly on the wax paper until ⅛″ thick. Turn the pastry over three or four times as you roll.
Stir together:
> ½ cup ground walnuts
> ¼ cup sifted icing sugar
> 1 teaspoon cinnamon

Spread the left half of each rectangle with walnut mixture.
Take hold of the right side of the pastry and lay it on top of the walnut mixture.
Use your rolling pin to roll pastry until ⅛″ thick.
Cut into strips ½″ wide. Use a tape measure ½″ wide as your guide.
Cut each strip into 7″ lengths.
Take hold of each end of a strip and make a bowtie shape, as in the drawing.

Place the bowties about 1″ apart on cookie pans.
Place the pans in the refrigerator.
Leave for 15 minutes.

Heat oven to 425°.

Bake one pan on the middle rack for about 10 minutes. (Let the other pan wait and cook later on the middle rack.)
Leave bowties on their pan.
Leave for 5 minutes on a cooling rack.
Remove bowties from their pan and return to the cooling rack for 10 minutes.
Dust with sifted icing sugar.

Pears in Overcoats

You need the basic recipe ingredients plus

> sugar
> pears, 6
> milk
> corn syrup
> brown sugar
> cinnamon
> butter, melted

Make this change to the basic recipe:
> Add 2 tablespoons sugar to the flour

Follow the basic technique until you have completed step 8 by hand or step 8 by food processor.

Now:
Dampen your table with water.
Lay two large pieces of wax paper on the table. (The water helps the wax paper to stick to the table.)
Dust the wax paper with flour.
Dust your rolling pin with flour.
Divide the pastry in half.
Use your rolling pin to roll pastry directly on the wax paper until 1/8″ thick. Turn the pastry over three or four times as you roll.
Cut into overcoat and scarf shapes. Use a wax paper pattern like the one on this page as your guide.
Take hold of each end of an overcoat and place over a pear, as in the drawing.
Squeeze the edges together on both sides and the bottom.

Place the pears about 2″ apart on an ungreased cookie pan (one with sides is perfect as this may dribble in the oven!)

Brush overcoats with milk.
Take hold of each end of a scarf and place around pear; press the scarf down firmly onto the overcoat.
Place the pan in the refrigerator.
Leave for 15 minutes.

Heat oven to 450°.
Bake pan on the middle rack for about 10 minutes.
Turn oven down to 375°.
Continue to bake pan for about 20 minutes.
Leave pears in their pan.
Leave for 5 minutes on a cooling rack.
Remove pears from their pan.

Stir together and cook for 5 minutes over medium heat:

> 1/3 cup water
> 2 tablespoons corn syrup
> 1 cup brown sugar
> 1/2 teaspoon cinnamon
> 1/3 cup butter

Serve this sauce with the pears.

Sausage Love Letters

You need the basic recipe ingredients plus

> dried basil or dill weed
> oil
> green pepper, chopped *or* spinach, chopped
> an onion, chopped
> Italian sausages, 8 cooked and chopped OR pork
> sausages, 8 cooked and chopped (remove the
> skins)
> mozzarella cheese, grated
> black pepper

Make this change to the basic recipe:

> Add 1 teaspoon crumbled basil or dill weed to the
> flour

Follow the basic technique until you have completed step 8 by hand or step 8 by food processor.

Now:
Choose a large frying pan.
Add 2 tablespoons of oil.
Cook for 5 minutes over medium heat:

> ⅓ cup chopped green pepper OR
> 1 cup chopped spinach
> ⅓ cup chopped onion

Add and stir together:

> chopped sausages
> 1 cup grated mozzarella
> ½ teaspoon pepper

Grease two cookie pans and dust with flour.
Dust your rolling pin with flour.
Divide the pastry in half.
Use your rolling pin to roll pastry directly on the pans until ⅛″ thick. Turn the pastry over three or four times as you roll.
Cut into rectangles 9″ x 15″. Use a ruler as your guide.
Spread one half of each rectangle with sausage mixture.
Take hold of the other half and lay it over the sausage mixture, as in the drawing.
See *What to Do with Edges* page 75.
Use a small knife to cut the initials of friends on the top of the love letters.
Place the pans in the refrigerator.
Leave for 15 minutes.

Heat oven to 450°.
Bake one pan on the lowest rack for about 10 minutes.
Turn oven down to 375°.
Continue to bake pan on the middle rack for about 10 minutes.
Let the other pan wait and cook later on the middle rack.
Leave love letters on their pan.
Leave for 5 minutes on a cooling rack.
Remove love letters from their pan and return to the cooling rack for 5 minutes.

Surprise Packages

You need the basic recipe ingredients plus

    lemon rind, finely grated
    1 large egg
    sugar
    cream cheese, room temperature
    vanilla
    icing sugar

Make this change to the basic recipe:

    Add 1 teaspoon grated lemon rind to the flour

Follow the basic technique until you have completed step 8 by hand or step 8 by food processor.

Now:
Stir together:

    2 tablespoons of egg
    ¼ cup sugar
    cream cheese, 4 ounces
    ½ teaspoon vanilla

Dampen your table with water.
Lay two large pieces of wax paper on the table. (The water helps the wax paper to stick to the table.)
Dust the wax paper with flour.
Dust your rolling pin with flour.
Divide the pastry in half.
Use your rolling pin to roll pastry directly on the wax paper until ⅛″ thick. Turn the pastry over three or four times as you roll.

Cut into squares 3″ x 3″. Use a wax paper pattern 3″ x 3″ as your guide.

Fit the pastry squares into muffin pans, as in the drawing.
Fill squares with 1 teaspoon of cheese mixture.
Take hold of two corners of the pastry square and squeeze firmly together, as in the drawing.
Squeeze the other two corners firmly together.
Place the pan in the refrigerator.
Leave for 15 minutes.

Heat oven to 450°.
Bake pan on the middle rack for about 10 minutes.
Turn oven down to 375°.
Continue to bake pan for about 10 minutes.
Leave surprise packages in their pan.
Leave for 5 minutes on a cooling rack.
Remove surprise packages from their pan and return to the cooling rack for 10 minutes.
Dust with sifted icing sugar.

Chocolate Bonbons

You need the basic recipe ingredients plus

  semi-sweet chocolate chips, 2 cups
  icing sugar

Follow the basic technique until you have completed step 8 by hand or step 8 by food processor.

Now:
Dampen your table with water.
Lay two large pieces of wax paper on the table. (The water helps the wax paper to stick to the table.)
Dust the wax paper with flour.
Dust your rolling pin with flour.
Divide the pastry in half.
Use your rolling pin to roll pastry directly on the wax paper until 1/8" thick. Turn the pastry over three or four times as you roll.
Cut into squares 4" x 4". Use a wax paper pattern 4" x 4" as your guide.
Spread squares with 1½ tablespoons of chocolate chips.
Take hold of one side of the pastry square and roll up to the other side, as in the drawing.

Place the rolls, with the seam down, about 1" apart on a cookie pan.
Twist each end, as in the drawing.
Place the pan in the refrigerator.
Leave for 15 minutes.

Heat oven to 450°.
Bake pan on the middle rack for about 10 minutes.
Turn oven down to 375°.
Continue to bake pan for about 5 minutes.
Leave bonbons on their pan.
Leave for 5 minutes on a cooling rack.
Remove bonbons from their pan and return to the cooling rack for 10 minutes.
Dust with sifted icing sugar.

Blueberry Squares

You need the basic recipe ingredients plus

>   lemon rind, finely grated
>   cornstarch
>   sugar
>   blueberries, 3 cups
>   milk

Make this change to the basic recipe:

>   Add 1 teaspoon grated lemon rind to the flour

Follow the basic technique until you have completed step 8 by hand or step 8 by food processor.

Now:
Stir together and cook for 5 minutes over medium heat:

>   1 tablespoon cornstarch mixed with ½ cup sugar
>   2 cups blueberries
>   ¼ cup water

Grease two cookie pans and dust with flour.
Dust your rolling pin with flour.
Divide the pastry in half.
Use your rolling pin to roll pastry directly on the pans until ⅛" thick. Turn the pastry over three or four times as you roll.
Cut into 10" squares.
Take hold of one corner of one square and lay it on top of the opposite corner, as in the drawing.
Cut 1" bands, as in the drawing. Use a ruler 1" wide as your guide.

Take hold of the top triangle and lay it back down on the cookie pan, as in the drawing.
Brush tops with milk.
Take hold of the right corner and lay it on top of the opposite corner.
Take hold of the left corner and lay it on top of the opposite corner, as in the drawing.
Use a fork to prick the bottom of the square. (This keeps the bottom of the pastry flat.)
Place the pans in the refrigerator.
Leave for 15 minutes.

Heat oven to 450°.
Bake one pan on the middle rack for about 10 minutes. (Let the other pan wait and cook later on the middle rack.)
Leave squares on their pan.
Leave for 5 minutes on a cooling rack.
Remove squares from their pan and return to the cooling rack for 10 minutes.
Fill squares with ½ cup of blueberries.
Spoon the cooked mixture over the blueberries in each square.

Chicken Pie

You need the basic recipe ingredients plus

    chicken, 6 pounds, cut up
    chicken broth, 2 cans (10 ounces)
    carrots, 4, sliced
    an onion, sliced
    peas or snow peas, 2 cups
    cream
    ginger
    butter

Follow the basic technique until you have completed step 8 by hand or step 8 by food processor.

Now:
Choose a large saucepan that can be used both on top of the stove and in the oven.
Place the chicken pieces in the saucepan.

Pour in the chicken broth, 2 cups water, carrots and onion.
Cook for 60 minutes over medium heat.
Pour in the peas.
Leave saucepan for 30 minutes on a cooling rack.

Now:
Grease two cookie pans and dust with flour.
Dust your rolling pin with flour.
Divide the pastry in half.
Use your rolling pin to roll pastry directly on the pans until ⅛″ thick. Turn the pastry over three or four times as you roll.
Choose a round serving dish for the chicken pie.
Cut the pastry into a 'flower' shape a little larger than the serving dish.
Place the pan in the refrigerator.
Leave for 15 minutes.
See *What to Do with Trimmings* page 75; and using the other pastry half, shape small flowers as directed.

Heat oven to 425°.
Bake pan on the middle rack for about 9 minutes.
Leave pastry on its pan.
Leave for 5 minutes on a cooling rack.
Remove pastry from its pan and return to the cooling rack.

Now:
Cut the chicken meat into bite size pieces, and return to the saucepan.
Add 1 cup cream.

Stir together and add:

    6 tablespoons flour
    1 teaspoon ginger
    6 tablespoons butter

Cook for 2 minutes, stirring constantly.

Heat oven to 400°.
Cover the saucepan.
Bake 25 minutes.
Uncover the saucepan.
Return pastry to cookie pan, place in oven with chicken mixture and bake both 8 minutes more.

Fill serving dish with chicken mixture and lay pastry 'flowers' on top, as in the drawing.

Banana Baskets

You need the basic recipe ingredients plus

    peanut butter
    dry white beans
    ripe bananas, 2 mashed
    sugar
    1 large egg
    almond extract
    whipping cream
    fine sugar (berry sugar is the same)
    peanuts, coarsely chopped

Make this change to the basic recipe:

    Add 1 tablespoon peanut butter to the lard

Follow the basic technique until you have completed step 8 by hand or step 8 by food processor.

Now:
Dampen your table with water.
Lay two large pieces of wax paper on the table. (The water helps the wax paper to stick to the table.)
Dust the wax paper with flour.
Dust your rolling pin with flour.
Divide the pastry in half.
Use your rolling pin to roll pastry directly on the wax paper until 1/8″ thick. Turn the pastry over three or four times as you roll.
Cut into squares 3½″ x 3½″. Use a wax paper pattern 3½″ x 3½″ as your guide.

Fit the pastry squares into muffin pans, as in the drawing.
Pour a few beans into each pastry square. (This keeps the bottom of the pastry flat.)
Place pan in the refrigerator.
Leave for 15 minutes.

Heat oven to 450°.
Bake pan on the lowest rack for about 8 minutes.
Leave baskets in their pan.
Leave for 5 minutes on a cooling rack.
Remove baskets from their pan; return to the cooling rack for 10 minutes and remove the beans. (Save the beans and use them again.)

Beat together until very thick, using an electric mixer:

    1 cup mashed bananas
    ½ cup sugar
    1/8 teaspoon salt
    1 egg white
    ¼ teaspoon almond extract

Return baskets to their pan.
Fill baskets with banana mixture.

Heat oven to 375°.
Bake pan on the middle rack for about 12 minutes.
Leave baskets in their pan.
Leave for 5 minutes on a cooling rack.
Remove baskets from their pan and return to the cooling rack for 10 minutes.

See *What to Do with Whipping Cream* page 75.
Spoon whipped cream on each basket.
Sprinkle with coarsely chopped peanuts.

Rum & Butter Baskets

You need the basic recipe ingredients plus

  walnuts, both finely chopped and coarsely
  chopped
  dry white beans
  raisins
  butter, melted
  brown sugar
  1 large egg
  rum or cream

Make this change to the basic recipe:

  Add 1 tablespoon finely chopped walnuts to the
  flour

Follow the basic technique until you have completed
step 8 by hand or step 8 by food processor.

Now:
Dampen your table with water.
Lay two large pieces of wax paper on the table. (The
water helps the wax paper to stick to the table.)
Dust the wax paper with flour.
Dust your rolling pin with flour.
Divide the pastry in half.
Use your rolling pin to roll pastry directly on the wax
paper until 1/8″ thick. Turn the pastry over three or
four times as you roll.
Cut into squares 3½″ x 3½″. Use a wax paper pattern
3½″ x 3½″as your guide.

Fit the pastry squares into muffin pans, as in the drawing.
Pour a few beans into each pastry square. (This keeps the bottom of the pastry flat.)
Place the pan in the refrigerator.
Leave for 15 minutes.
Remove the trimmings and squeeze into a ball. See *What to Do with Trimmings* page 75 and shape small hearts as directed.

Heat oven to 450°.
Bake pan on the lowest rack for about 8 minutes.
Leave baskets in their pan.
Leave for 5 minutes on a cooling rack.
Remove baskets from their pan; return to the cooling rack for 10 minutes and remove the beans. (Save the beans and use them again.)

Stir together ½ cup raisins and ¼ cup coarsely chopped walnuts.
Return baskets to their pan.
Fill baskets with 1 teaspoon of raisin mixture.

Stir together:

   ¼ cup melted butter, cooled
   ¾ cup brown sugar
   1 large egg, beaten
   1 tablespoon rum or cream

Fill baskets ⅔ full with egg mixture.
Heat oven to 375°.
Bake pan on the middle rack for about 12 minutes.
Leave baskets in their pan.
Leave for 5 minutes on a cooling rack.
Remove baskets from their pan and return to the cooling rack for 10 minutes.

Lay baked hearts on each basket.

Cream Horns

You need the basic equipment plus

    metal horn molds, 4" x 1½"

You need the basic recipe ingredients plus:

    whipping cream
    fine sugar (berry sugar is the same)
    chocolate sprinkles

Follow the basic technique until you have completed step 8 by hand or step 8 by food processor.

Now:
Dampen your table with water.
Lay two large pieces of wax paper on the table. (The water helps the wax paper to stick to the table.)
Dust the wax paper with flour.
Dust your rolling pin with flour.
Divide the pastry in half.
Use your rolling pin to roll pastry directly on the wax paper until ⅛" thick. Turn the pastry over three or four times as you roll.
Cut into strips 1" wide. Use a ruler 1" wide as your guide.
Cut each strip into a 14" length.
Take hold of each end of a strip and wind around a horn mold; beginning at the tip of the mold and overlapping the strips about ½", as in the drawing.

Place the horns with the seam down about 1" apart on a dampened cookie pan.
Place the pan in the refrigerator.
Leave for 15 minutes.

Heat oven to 450°.
Bake pan on the middle rack for about 10 minutes.
Turn oven down to 375°.
Continue to bake pan for about 5 minutes.
Leave horns on their pan.
Leave for 5 minutes on a cooling rack.
Remove horns from their pan; remove metal molds and return horns to the cooling rack for 10 minutes.

See *What to Do with Whipping Cream,* page 75.
Fill horns with whipped cream.
Sprinkle whipped cream with chocolate sprinkles, as in the drawing.

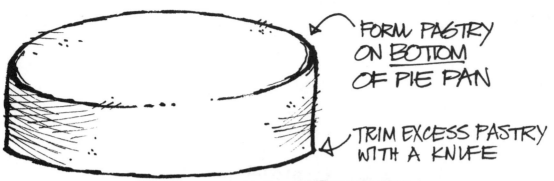

FORM PASTRY ON BOTTOM OF PIE PAN

TRIM EXCESS PASTRY WITH A KNIFE

Raspberry Heart

You need the basic recipe ingredients plus

> 3 large egg yolks
> cornstarch
> sugar
> cream
> almond liqueur or cherry brandy
> raspberries, 2 cups

Follow the basic technique until you have completed step 8 by hand or step 8 by food processor.

Now:
Dampen your table with water.
Lay two large pieces of wax paper on the table. (The water helps the wax paper to stick to the table.)
Dust the wax paper with flour.
Dust your rolling pin with flour.
Divide the pastry in half.
Use your rolling pin to roll pastry directly on the wax paper until 1/8" thick. Turn the pastry over three or four times as you roll.

Choose an 8" or 9" pie pan.
Turn the pan upside down on the table.
Take hold of one wax paper with the pastry on it.
Lay the pastry on the pie pan and peel the wax paper off, as in the drawing.
Cut away the extra pastry.
Use a fork to prick the pastry. (This keeps the pastry flat.)
Place the pan in the refrigerator.
Leave for 15 minutes.
See *What to Do with Trimmings* page 75; and using the other pastry half, shape hearts as directed.

Heat oven to 450°.
Bake pan on the lowest rack for about 10 minutes.
Leave pastry shell on its pan.
Leave for 5 minutes on a cooling rack.
Remove pastry shell from its pan and return to the cooling rack for 10 minutes.

Stir together until smooth:

> 3 large egg yolks
> 2 tablespoons cornstarch
> 1/3 cup sugar

Cook for 10 minutes over low heat in a thick bottomed saucepan, stirring constantly:

> 1 cup cream, warm
> 3 tablespoons almond liqueur or cherry brandy
> the egg yolk mixture

Fill shell with mixture.
Arrange the raspberries in a heart shape over the cream mixture, as in the drawing.

Lay baked hearts around the pie, as in the drawing.

Twin Berry Pie

You need the basic recipe ingredients plus

    fennel seeds, crushed
    cornstarch
    sugar
    butter, soft
    blueberries or blackberries, 2 cups
    raspberries or strawberries, 2 cups

Follow the basic technique until you have completed step 8 by hand or step 8 by food processor.

Now:
Dampen your table with water.
Lay two large pieces of wax paper on the table. (The water helps the wax paper to stick to the table.)
Dust the wax paper with flour.
Dust your rolling pin with flour.
Divide the pastry in half.
Use your rolling pin to roll pastry directly on the wax paper until 1/8″ thick. Turn the pastry over three or four times as you roll.

Choose an 8″ or 9″ pie pan.
Take hold of one wax paper with the pastry on it.
Lay the pastry in the pie pan and peel the wax paper off.

Stir together:

    1 teaspoon crushed fennel seeds
    3 tablespoons cornstarch
    3/4 cup sugar
    2 tablespoons soft butter

Place the blueberries and raspberries in separate bowls.
Sprinkle 1/2 of the sugar mixture over the blueberries; sprinkle the rest of the mixture over the raspberries. Stir.

Fill one half of the circle in the pie pan with blueberry mixture.
Take hold of the other half of the circle and lay it on top of the blueberries, as in the drawing.
See *What to Do with Edges* page 75.
Lay the other circle in the pie pan and peel the wax paper off.
Fill half of the circle in the pie pan with raspberry mixture.
Take hold of the other half of the pastry circle and lay it on top of the raspberries, as in the drawing.
Use a small knife to cut a 'B' on the top of the blueberry part of the twin pie; cut an 'R' on the top of the raspberry part, as in the drawing.
Place the pan in the refrigerator.
Leave for 15 minutes.

Place a cookie pan on the middle oven rack.
Heat oven to 450°.
Place pie on the cookie pan. (The cookie pan helps the bottom of the pie to cook completely.)
Bake pie for about 18 minutes.
Turn oven down to 350°.
Continue to bake pie for about 45 minutes.
Leave pie in its pan.
Leave for 15 minutes on a cooling rack.

Whole Apple Pie

You need the basic recipe ingredients plus

    nutmeg
    walnuts, coarsely chopped
    McIntosh apples, 6
    sugar
    lemon juice
    cinnamon
    brown sugar
    butter, melted
    corn syrup

Make this change to the basic recipe:

    Add ½ teaspoon nutmeg to the flour

Follow the basic technique until you have completed step 8 by hand or step 8 by food processor.

Now:
Dampen your table with water.
Lay two large pieces of wax paper on the table. (The water helps the wax paper to stick to the table.)
Dust the wax paper with flour.
Dust your rolling pin with flour.
Divide the pastry in half.
Use your rolling pin to roll pastry directly on the wax paper ⅛″ thick. Turn the pastry over three or four times as you roll.

Choose an 8″ or 9″ pie pan.
Turn the pan upside down on the table.
Take hold of one wax paper with the pastry on it.
Lay the pastry on the pie pan and peel the wax paper off (see drawing on page 50).

Cut away the extra pastry.

Use a fork to prick the pastry. (This keeps the pastry flat.)

Place the pan in the refrigerator.

Leave for 15 minutes.

See *What to Do with Trimmings* page 75; and using the other pastry half, shape small hearts or stars as directed.

Heat oven to 450°.

Bake pan on the lowest rack for about 10 minutes.

Leave pastry shell on its pan.

Leave for 5 minutes on a cooling rack.

Remove pastry shell from its pan and place shell on a serving dish, right side up.

Fill shell with 1 cup coarsely chopped walnuts.

Cook for 5 minutes over medium heat, in a large pot:

6 peeled McIntosh apples with the stems left on
4 cups water
2 cups sugar
1 tablespoon lemon juice

Fill shell with apples, as in the drawing.

Stir together and cook for 5 minutes over medium heat:

½ teaspoon cinnamon
1 cup brown sugar
⅓ cup melted butter
2 tablespoons corn syrup
⅓ cup water

Drizzle this sauce over the pie.

Birthday Pie

You need the basic recipe ingredients plus

    orange juice
    whipping cream
    semisweet chocolate, 5 one ounce squares
    butter
    1 large egg
    vanilla
    icing sugar

Make this change to the basic recipe:

    Use orange juice rather than water

Follow the basic technique until you have completed step 8 by hand or step 8 by food processor. Repeat the basic technique; this gives you two 'hamburgers' of pastry.

Now:
Grease two cookie pans and dust with flour.
Dust your rolling pin with flour.
Divide each pastry 'hamburger' into 3 parts.
Wrap four of the pastry parts in wax paper.
Use your rolling pin to roll two of the pastry parts directly on the pans until ⅛″ thick. Turn the pastry over three or four times as you roll.
Cut into circles 9″ across. (Use a plate 9″ across as your guide.)
Use a fork to prick the top of the circles. (This keeps the pastry flat.)
Place the pans in the refrigerator.
Leave for 15 minutes.

Heat oven to 450°.
Bake one pan on the middle rack for about 10 minutes. (Let the other pan wait and cook later on the middle rack.)
Leave circle on its pan.
Leave for 5 minutes on a cooling rack.
Remove circle from its pan and return to the cooling rack for 10 minutes.

Roll and bake the other four pastry parts.

Stir together and heat for 2 or 3 minutes over very low heat in a thick bottomed saucepan:

> 1/4 cup whipping cream
> 2 squares semisweet chocolate, chopped
> 3 tablespoons butter
> 1/4 teaspoon salt

Let this mixture sit and cool for 20 minutes or so.
Beat together for 3 minutes, using an electric mixer on high:

> the cooled chocolate mixture
> 1 large egg
> 1 teaspoon vanilla

Continue to beat the chocolate mixture and add 2 cups sifted icing sugar.
Spread five of the circles with chocolate icing; saving some for the sixth circle.
Lay the circles one on top of another, as in the drawing.

Spread the sixth circle with chocolate icing, as in the drawing. Place this circle on top.

Stir and heat for 2 or 3 minutes over very low heat in a thick bottomed saucepan 3 squares of semisweet chocolate, chopped.
Lay a large piece of wax paper on a cookie pan.
Pour the melted chocolate onto the wax paper; lay a piece of wax paper on top of the chocolate.
Use your rolling pin to roll chocolate until it is 1/8" thick.

Place the pan in the refrigerator.
Leave for 12 minutes.
Peel off the top layer of wax paper.
Cut chocolate into small shapes with cookie cutters.
Peel the bottom layer of wax paper off the chocolate shapes.

Lay chocolate shapes on top of the pie, as in the drawing.
Place the pie in the refrigerator.
Leave for about 1 hour.

Upside Down Pie

You need the basic recipe ingredients plus

   butter, soft
   sugar
   apples, 6 large
   cinnamon
   nutmeg

Follow the basic technique until you have completed step 8 by hand or step 8 by food processor.

Now:
Dampen your table with water.
Lay two large pieces of wax paper on the table. (The water helps the wax paper to stick to the table.)
Dust the wax paper with flour.
Dust your rolling pin with flour.
Divide the pastry in half.
Use your rolling pin to roll pastry directly on the wax paper until 1/8″ thick. Turn the pastry over three or four times as you roll.

Choose an 8″ or 9″ pie pan.
Spread over the bottom and sides of the pie pan 2 tablespoons soft butter.
Stir together and cook until thick over medium heat:

   6 tablespoons sugar
   1 tablespoon butter

Pour the sugar mixture into the pie pan.

Stir together:

   6 large peeled, sliced apples
   1/2 teaspoon cinnamon
   1/4 teaspoon nutmeg

Fill pan with apple mixture.

Take hold of one wax paper with the pastry on it.
Lay the pastry on the pie pan and peel the wax paper off.
See *What to Do with Edges* page 75.
Use a small knife to cut several lines on the top of the upside down pie, as in the drawing.
Place the pan in the refrigerator.
Leave for 15 minutes.
See *What to Do with Trimmings* page 75; and using the other pastry half, shape small hearts or stars as directed.

Heat oven to 450°.
Bake pan on the middle rack for about 12 minutes.
Turn oven down to 375°.
Continue to bake pan for about 40 minutes.
Leave pie in its pan.
Leave for 60 minutes on a cooling rack.
Place a serving dish on top of the pie; quickly turn pie and dish over.
Remove pie pan.

Open Faced Raisin Pie

You need the basic recipe ingredients plus

> dry white beans
> raisins
> sugar
> lemon juice
> butter, melted
> brown sugar
> corn syrup
> heavy cream
> rum, if you wish

Follow the basic technique until you have completed step 8 by hand or step 8 by food processor.

Now:
Dampen your table with water.
Lay two large pieces of wax paper on the table. (The water helps the wax paper to stick to the table.)
Dust the wax paper with flour.
Dust your rolling pin with flour.
Divide the pastry in half.
Use your rolling pin to roll pastry directly on the wax paper until ⅛" thick. Turn the pastry over three or four times as you roll.

Choose an 8" or 9" pie pan.
Take hold of one wax paper with the pastry on it.
Lay the pastry in the pie pan and peel the wax paper off.
See *What to Do with Edges* page 75.

Pour a few beans into the pie pan. (This keeps the bottom of the pastry flat.)
Place the pan in the refrigerator.
Leave for 15 minutes.
See *What to Do with Trimmings* page 75; and using the other pastry half, shape small hearts or stars as directed.

Heat oven to 450°.
Bake pan on the lowest rack for about 5 minutes.
Leave pastry shell in its pan.
Leave for 10 minutes on a cooling rack and remove the beans. (Save the beans and use them again.)

Stir together and cook for 4 minutes:

  2 cups raisins
  1½ cups water

Stir together and slowly add to the raisin mixture:

  ½ cup sugar
  2 tablespoons flour

Cook for 5 minutes over low heat, stirring constantly.
Leave for 5 minutes on a cooling rack.
Add ¼ cup lemon juice to the raisin mixture; stir.
Fill shell with raisin mixture.

Heat oven to 375°.
Bake pie for about 25 minutes.
Leave pie in its pan.
Leave for 20 minutes on a cooling rack.

Stir together and cook for 1 minute over low heat:

  ⅓ cup melted butter
  1 cup brown sugar
  2 tablespoons corn syrup
  ⅓ cup heavy cream

Let this mixture sit and cool for 20 minutes or so.
If you wish, add 2 tablespoons of rum to the mixture.
Serve this sauce with the pie.

Lay baked hearts or stars around the pie, as in the drawing.

Brown Bag Apple Pie

You need the basic recipe ingredients plus

  dry white beans
  apples, 6 large
  sugar
  cinnamon
  nutmeg

Follow the basic technique until you have completed step 8 by hand or step 8 by food processor.

Now:
Dampen your table with water.
Lay two pieces of wax paper on the table. (The water helps the wax paper to stick to the table.)
Dust the wax paper with flour.
Dust your rolling pin with flour.
Divide the pastry in half.
Use your rolling pin to roll pastry directly on the wax paper until 1/8″ thick. Turn the pastry over three or four times as you roll.

Choose an 8″ or 9″ pie pan.
Take hold of one wax paper with the pastry on it.
Lay the pastry in the pie pan and peel the wax paper off.
Press the edges into a fancy shape. See *What to Do with Edges* page 75.
Pour a few beans into the pie pan. (This keeps the bottom of the pastry flat.)
Place the pan in the refrigerator.
Leave for 15 minutes.
See *What to Do with Trimmings* page 75; and using the other pastry half, shape small hearts or stars as directed.

Heat oven to 450°.
Bake pan on the lowest rack for about 8 minutes.
Leave pastry shell in its pan.
Leave for 10 minutes on a cooling rack and remove the beans. (Save the beans and use them again.)

Stir together:

  6 large peeled, sliced apples
  1/2 cup sugar
  1 tablespoon flour
  1/2 teaspoon cinnamon
  1/4 teaspoon nutmeg

Fill shell with apple mixture.
Place pan in a brown grocery bag. Tuck the open end of the bag under the pan. Place bag on a cookie pan.

Heat oven to 425°.
Bake pan on the middle rack for about 40 minutes.
Remove the brown bag.
Leave the pie in its pan.
Leave for 10 minutes on a cooling rack.

Lay baked hearts or stars around the pie, as in the drawing.

Peanut Butter Pie

You need the basic recipe ingredients plus

unflavored gelatin
3 large eggs
sugar
peanut butter
vanilla
whipping cream
fine sugar (berry sugar is the same)

Follow the basic technique until you have completed step 8 by hand or step 8 by food processor.

Now:
Dampen your table with water.
Lay two large pieces of wax paper on the table. (The water helps the wax paper to stick to the table.)
Dust the wax paper with flour.
Dust your rolling pin with flour.
Divide the pastry in half.
Use your rolling pin to roll pastry directly on the wax paper until ⅛″ thick. Turn the pastry over three or four times as you roll.

Choose an 8″ or 9″ pie pan.
Turn the pan upside down on the table.
Take hold of one wax paper with the pastry on it.
Lay the pastry on the pie pan and peel the wax paper off (see drawing on page 50).
Cut away the extra pastry.
Use a fork to prick the pastry. (This keeps the pastry flat.)
Place the pan in the refrigerator.
Leave for 15 minutes.
See *What to Do with Trimmings* page 75; and using the other pastry half, shape hearts or peanuts as directed.

Heat oven to 450°.
Bake pan on the lowest rack for about 10 minutes.
Leave pastry shell on its pan.
Leave for 5 minutes on a cooling rack.
Remove pastry shell from its pan and return to the cooling rack for 10 minutes.

Sprinkle 1 envelope of gelatin over ¼ cup of cold water.
Leave this gelatin mixture for 5 minutes and then stir.
Stir together in the top part of a double boiler:

3 large egg yolks
2 tablespoons sugar
½ cup water
½ teaspoon salt
the gelatin mixture

Fill the bottom part of the double boiler half full with water. Heat the water until it is gently boiling.
Place the top part of the double boiler over the bottom part. Return the boiler to the stove over medium heat.
Beat the mixture in the top of the boiler for about 5 minutes, using an electric mixer on medium. (The mixture will now be thick and fluffy.)
Let this mixture sit and cool for 20 minutes or so.

Stir together and add to the gelatin mixture:

½ cup peanut butter
¾ cup water
½ teaspoon vanilla

Stir; cover and let this mixture cool in the refrigerator for about 40 minutes. (The mixture will be thick now like a milk shake.) If it's not thick, stir and return to the refrigerator for about another 20 minutes.

Choose a small bowl.
Pour into the bowl 3 egg whites.
Beat the whites for about 2 minutes, using an electric mixer on medium. (The whites will be a white color now.)
Sprinkle the whites with 2 tablespoons of sugar.
Beat the whites for about another 5 minutes, using the mixer on high. (The whites will be very thick looking now.)
Stir the whites *very gently* into the cold peanut butter mixture.
Fill shell with peanut butter mixture.
Cover the pie and place in the refrigerator.
See *What to Do with Whipping Cream* page 75.
Spoon whipped cream onto the pie.
Lay baked hearts or peanuts around the pie, as in the drawing.

Pumpkin Face Pie

You need the basic recipe ingredients plus

> cinnamon
> unflavored gelatin
> canned pumpkin
> heavy cream
> brown sugar
> 3 large eggs
> ginger
> nutmeg
> whipping cream
> fine sugar (berry sugar is the same)

Make this change to the basic recipe:

> Add ½ teaspoon cinnamon to the flour

Follow the basic technique until you have completed step 8 by hand or step 8 by food processor.

Now:
Dampen your table with water.
Lay two pieces of wax paper on the table. (The water helps the wax paper to stick to the table.)
Dust the wax paper with flour.
Dust your rolling pin with flour.
Divide the pastry in half.
Use your rolling pin to roll pastry directly on the wax paper until ⅛″ thick. Turn the pastry over three or four times as you roll.

Choose an 8″ or 9″ pie pan.
Turn the pan upside down on the table.
Take hold of one wax paper with the pastry on it.
Lay the pastry on the pie pan and peel the wax paper off (see drawing on page 50).

Cut away the extra pastry.

Use a fork to prick the pastry. (This keeps the pastry flat.)

Place the pan in the refrigerator.

Leave for 15 minutes.

See *What to Do with Trimmings* page 75; and using the other pastry half, shape a pumpkin as directed. Use a wax paper pattern like the one on this page as your guide.

Use a fork to 'draw' in his face.

Heat oven to 450°.

Bake pan on the lowest rack for about 10 minutes.

Leave pastry shell on its pan.

Leave for 5 minutes on a cooling rack.

Remove pastry shell from its pan and return to the cooling rack for 10 minutes.

Sprinkle 1 envelope of gelatin over ¼ cup of cold water.

Leave this gelatin mixture for 5 minutes and then stir.

Cook for 10 minutes over low heat in a thick bottomed saucepan, stirring constantly:

   1½ cups canned pumpkin
   ½ cup heavy cream
   ½ cup brown sugar
   3 beaten egg yolks
   ¾ teaspoon cinnamon
   ¾ teaspoon ginger
   ¼ teaspoon nutmeg
   ¼ teaspoon salt
   the gelatin mixture

Let this mixture sit and cool for 20 minutes or so.

Choose a small bowl.

Pour into the bowl 3 egg whites.

Beat the whites for about 2 minutes, using an electric mixer on medium. (The whites will be a white color now.)

Sprinkle the whites with 2 tablespoons of sugar.

Beat the whites for another minute.

Sprinkle with 2 more tablespoons of sugar.

Beat the whites for about another 4 minutes, using the mixer on high. (The whites will be very thick looking now.)

Stir the whites *very gently* into the cold pumpkin mixture.

Fill shell with pumpkin mixture.

Cover the pie and place in the refrigerator.

See *What to Do with Whipping Cream*, page 75.

Lay the pumpkin face on the pie, as in the drawing.

Serve the whipped cream with the pie.

Onion & Bacon Pie

You need the basic recipe ingredients plus

    dried basil or dill weed
    white wine
    dry white beans
    butter
    onions
    bacon, 1/2 pound, cooked and crumbled
    mozzarella cheese, grated
    Worcestershire sauce
    1 large egg
    black pepper

Make these changes to the basic recipe:

    Add 1 teaspoon crumbled basil or dill weed to the flour
    Use white wine rather than water

Follow the basic technique until you have completed step 8 by hand or step 8 by food processor.

Now:
Dampen your table with water.
Lay two large pieces of wax paper on the table. (The water helps the wax paper to stick to the table.)
Dust the wax paper with flour.
Dust your rolling pin with flour.
Divide the pastry in half.
Use your rolling pin to roll pastry directly on the wax paper until 1/8" thick. Turn the pastry over three or four times as you roll.

Choose an 8" or 9" pie pan.
Take hold of one wax paper with the pastry on it.
Lay the pastry in the pie pan and peel the wax paper off.
See *What to Do with Edges* page 75.
Pour a few beans into the pie pan. (This keeps the bottom of the pastry flat.)

Place the pan in the refrigerator.
Leave for 15 minutes.
See *What to Do with Trimmings* page 75; and using the other pastry half, shape half circles as directed.

Heat oven to 450°.
Bake pan on the middle rack for about 8 minutes.
Leave pastry shell in its pan.
Leave for 10 minutes on a cooling rack and remove the beans. (Save the beans and use them again.)

Choose a large frying pan.
Add 3 tablespoons of butter.
Over low heat cook 4 cups sliced onions. (This will take about 20 minutes.)

Stir together:

    crumbled bacon
    cooked onions
    1 1/4 cups grated mozzarella
    1 teaspoon Worcestershire sauce
    1 beaten egg
    1/2 teaspoon pepper

Fill shell with onion mixture.
Lay the half circles around the pie, as in the drawing.

Place a cookie pan on the middle oven rack.
Heat oven to 375°.
Place pie on the cookie pan. (The cookie pan helps the bottom of the pie to cook completely.)
Bake pie for about 35 minutes.
Leave pie in its pan.
Leave for 5 minutes on a cooling rack.

Chocolate Strawberry Baskets

You need the basic recipe ingredients plus

  dry white beans
  3 large eggs
  cornstarch
  sugar
  cream
  semisweet chocolate, 3 one ounce squares
  vanilla
  strawberries

Follow the basic technique until you have completed step 8 by hand or step 8 by food processor.

Now:
Dampen your table with water.
Lay two large pieces of wax paper on the table. (The water helps the wax paper to stick to the table.)
Dust the wax paper with flour.
Dust your rolling pin with flour.
Divide the pastry in half.
Use your rolling pin to roll pastry directly on the wax paper until $1/8''$ thick. Turn the pastry over three or four times as you roll.
Cut the rectangle into squares $3^1/2'' \times 3^1/2''$. Use a wax paper pattern $3^1/2'' \times 3^1/2''$ as your guide.

Fit the pastry squares into muffin pans.
Pour a few beans into each pastry square. (This keeps the bottom of the pastry flat.)
Place the pan in the refrigerator.
Leave for 15 minutes.

Heat oven to 450°.
Bake pan on the middle rack for about 10 minutes.
Leave baskets in their pan.
Leave for 5 minutes on a cooling rack.
Remove baskets from their pan; return to the cooling rack for 10 minutes and remove the beans. (Save the beans and use them again.)

Stir together until smooth:

  3 large egg yolks
  2 tablespoons cornstarch
  $1/3$ cup sugar

Cook for 10 minutes over low heat in a thick bottomed saucepan, stirring constantly: the egg yolk mixture and 1 cup warm cream.

Chop the chocolate into small pieces.
Add the chocolate pieces and $1/2$ teaspoon vanilla to the egg mixture; stir until all the chocolate has melted.

Fill baskets with 1 tablespoon of chocolate mixture.
Cover the baskets and place in the refrigerator.

Arrange one or two strawberries in each basket, as in the drawing.

Watermelon Round

You need the basic recipe ingredients plus

> sugar
> 2 large eggs
> butter, soft
> almonds, ground
> watermelon
> cornstarch
> apple juice

Make this change to the basic recipe:

> Add 2 tablespoons sugar to the flour

Follow the basic technique until you have completed step 8 by hand or step 8 by food processor.

Now:
Grease two cookie pans and dust with flour.
Dust your rolling pin with flour.
Divide the pastry in half.
Use your rolling pin to roll pastry directly on the pans until ⅛" thick. Turn the pastry over three or four times as you roll.
Cut one into a circle 9" across. Use a plate 9" across as your guide.
Use a fork to prick the top of the circle. (This keeps the pastry flat.)
Cut the second into strips ¼" wide. Use a ruler as your guide.
Take hold of three strips about the same length.
Braid the 3 parts together.
Squeeze the ends together.

Lay braids around the edge of the pastry circle, as in the drawing. (It is a help to brush the edge of the pastry circle with water to help 'glue' the braids on.)
Place the pan in the refrigerator.
Leave for 15 minutes.

Heat oven to 450°.
Bake pan on the middle rack for about 10 minutes.
Leave circle on its pan.
Leave for 5 minutes on a cooling rack.
Remove circle from its pan and return to the cooling rack for 10 minutes.

Choose a small bowl.
Pour into the bowl 2 egg yolks.
Beat yolks for about 3 minutes, using an electric mixer on high.
Beat together and add to the egg yolks:

   2 tablespoons soft butter
   ⅓ cup sugar
   ¼ cup ground almonds

Return round to its pan.
Fill round with almond mixture.
Heat oven to 400°.
Bake round on the lowest rack for about 10 minutes.
Leave round on its pan.
Leave for 5 minutes on a cooling rack.
Remove round from its pan and return to the cooling rack for 10 minutes.

Cut the watermelon into ¼" thick triangles.
Remove the seeds.
Arrange the slices on the round, as in the drawing.
Stir together:

   ½ cup sugar
   1 tablespoon cornstarch

Cook for 5 minutes over medium heat, stirring constantly:

   the sugar mixture
   1 cup apple juice

Spoon this apple glaze over the watermelon.
Cover the round and place in the refrigerator.

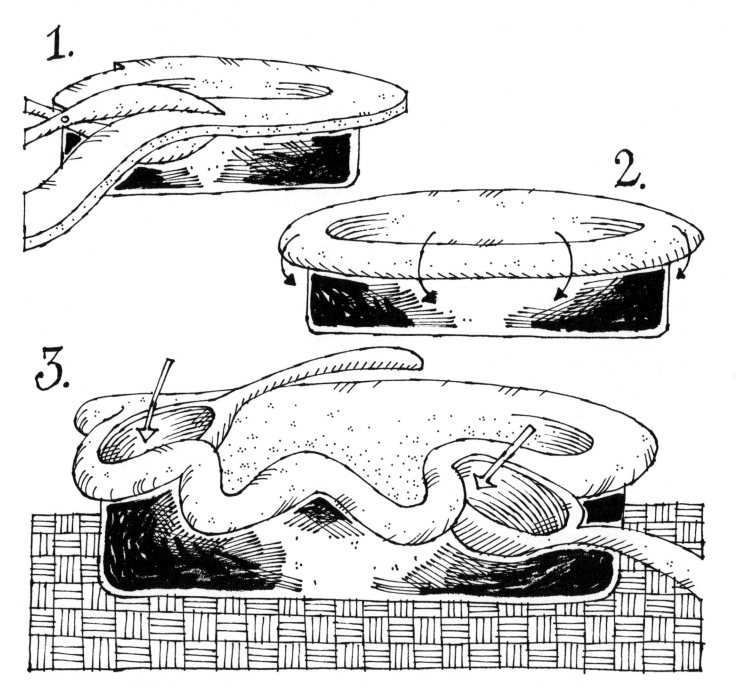

1.

2.

3.

What to Do with Trimmings

Gather the trimmings and squeeze into a ball.
Flatten the ball into a hamburger shape.
Wrap in wax paper.
Place in the refrigerator.
Leave for ½ hour
or leave overnight.

Grease a cookie pan and dust with flour.
Dust your rolling pin with flour.
Leave the pastry for 40 minutes on the table if it was in the refrigerator overnight.
Use your hands to flatten the hamburger shape until it is ½" thick.
Use your rolling pin to roll pastry directly on the cookie pan until it is ⅛" thick.
or if you have already rolled the pastry on wax paper, pull the wax paper onto a cookie pan and continue.
Cut into shapes with cookie cutters.
(Cut the shapes about 2" apart as they 'grow' in the oven!)
Place the pan in the refrigerator.
Leave for 15 minutes.

Heat oven to 425°.
Brush the shapes with milk and sprinkle quickly with sugar and cinnamon
or brush the shapes with soft butter and sprinkle with dried dill or basil.
Bake pan on the middle rack for about 10 minutes.
Leave shapes on their pan.
Leave for 5 minutes on a cooling rack.
Remove shapes from their pan and return to the cooling rack for 10 minutes.

What to Do with Edges

Use scissors to cut the pastry hanging over the pie pan until it is about 1" wide, as in the drawing.
Fold this 1" of pastry in half making a thick ½" edge, as in the drawing.
Shape the edge using a tablespoon, as in the drawing.

What to Do with Whipping Cream

Choose a small bowl.
Place the bowl in the refrigerator.
Leave for 15 minutes.
Pour 1 cup of whipping cream into the bowl.
Beat the cream for about 1 minute, using an electric mixer on high. (The cream will now be foamy.)
Sprinkle 2 tablespoons of fine sugar into the cream mixture.
Continue to beat the cream for about another 2 minutes. (The cream will now be very thick.)

Refrigerate the whipped cream.

About the Author & Illustrator

Donna Thacker graduated from the University of Alberta (Nutrition and Applied Design) in 1965. She taught textiles for five years. When her two children were small and she couldn't find bright and happy clothing designs for them, she created her own. Woodwards Stores in Western Canada saw her do-it-yourself ladybug dress kit and giant pinwheel overalls and marketed them.

When she taught foods she guided beginners from the easy steps of basic bread and pastry to unexpected shapes and sizes of her own creation: *Pears in Overcoats, Watermelon Rounds* and *Bowties*.

Canadian Living's food editor Carol Ferguson said of Donna's first book *Bread Without Tears* (1983):

> "For the simplest possible recipe for making a lovely, fat loaf, look for a bright new book called *Bread Without Tears*. From one very easy, basic recipe she gives techniques for mixing by hand, by electric mixer with a dough hook and by food processor. She then proceeds to all sorts of shaping and flavoring variations. Donna believes in happy cooking, and the charming illustrations by David Shaw will also cheer you up."

David Shaw was born in London, England and came to Canada at age six. In 1969, he graduated from the Ontario College of Art. He has designed over 700 books including *The Canadian Encyclopedia*.

Donna chose David Shaw as illustrator for her second book, *Pastry Without Tears* because "illustrations should be as friendly as a visitor in your kitchen."

Designed and illustrated by David Shaw
Edited by Patricia McColl Bee
Composed in Zapf Book by Accurate Typesetting Ltd.
Author photograph by Phillip Mirsky
Manufactured in Altona, Manitoba by
D.W. Friesen & Sons

First edition, 1986